Stories by Significant Aut

selected by Wendy Body

Contents

Section 1
Ben Biggins' Tummy Judith Nicholls … 2
Mrs Plug and the Robber Allan Ahlberg … 4
From *Mrs Plug the Plumber*

Section 2
The Story of Miss Moppet Beatrix Potter … 8
From *More Tales by Beatrix Potter*
The Giant Wakes Martin Waddell … 12
From *Man Mountain*

Section 3
The Monster Appears Gene Kemp … 16
From *Matty's Midnight Monster*
Clever Polly Catherine Storr … 20
From *Clever Polly and the Stupid Wolf*

Glossary of Verbs … 24

Longman

Edinburgh Gate
Harlow, Essex

Ben Biggins' Tummy

"I'm hungry!" yelled Ben Biggins.

"Do you want some peas?" asked Mum.

"No!" yelled Ben.

"No **thank you**!" said Mum.

"Do you want some chips?" asked Dad.

"No!" yelled Ben Biggins.

"No **thank you**!" said Dad.

"Do you want some cabbage?" asked Jamila.

"NO!" yelled Ben Biggins.

"No **thank you**!" said Jamila.

"Are you really hungry?" asked Dad.

"Do you want some ice-cream?" asked Mum

"Yes!" yelled Ben Biggins.

"Yes **please**!" yelled everyone.

But Mum said ...

"**No**!"

From *Ben Biggins' Tummy*

by Judith Nicholls

Mrs Plug and the Robber

Mrs Plug had a useful bag. It had a saw, a hammer, a spanner, a pair of pliers, a purse, a comb, a lipstick, a plunger, a blow-lamp and a few other things in it.

One night there was some trouble in a lady's bathroom. A plumber was needed.

The neighbours said, "Send for Mrs Plug!"

Mrs Plug got on with the job. The lady gave her a cup of tea. When she had finished the lady gave her some money. Mrs Plug set off home.

On the way, a terrible thing happened. Mrs Plug saw a robber. He was robbing a rich man in the street. The robber saw Mrs Plug. He wanted to rob her too.

"What's in that bag?" he said.

"There's a comb," said Mrs Plug.

"I will have that!" said the robber.

"And a lipstick," said Mrs Plug.

"I will have that!" said the robber.

"And ... a ... blow-lamp!" said Mrs Plug.

Mrs Plug chased the robber with the blow-lamp. She burnt his bottom.

"Wow!" the robber shouted.

And he ran off.

**From *Mrs Plug the Plumber*
by Allan Ahlberg**

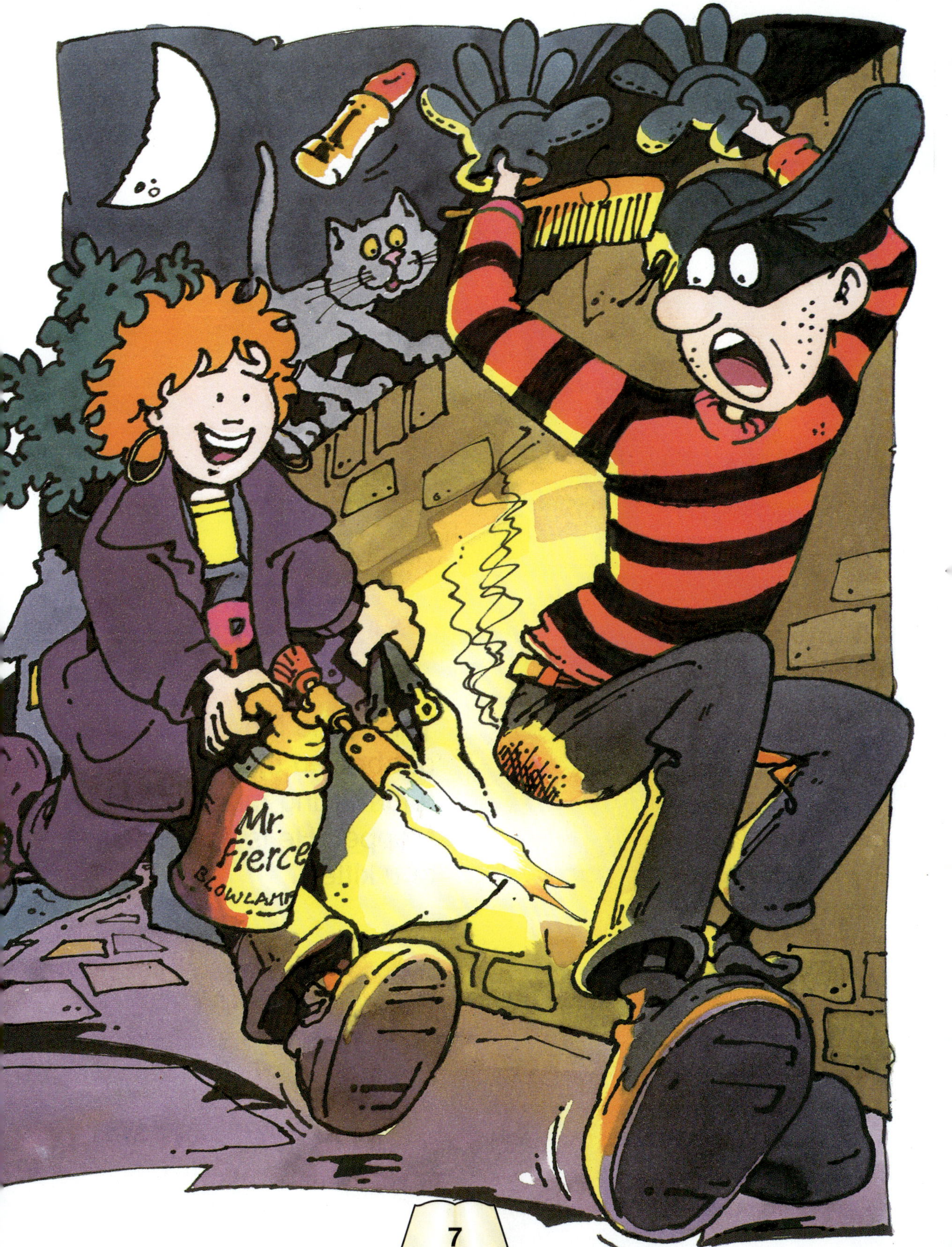
Mr. Fierce
BLOWLAMP

The Story of Miss Moppet

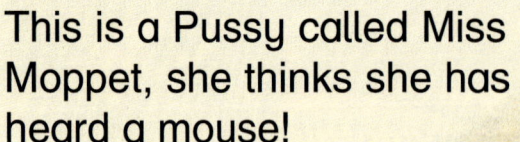

This is a Pussy called Miss Moppet, she thinks she has heard a mouse!

This is the Mouse peeping out behind the cupboard, and making fun of Miss Moppet. He is not afraid of a kitten.

This is Miss Moppet jumping just too late; she misses the Mouse and hits her own head. She thinks it is a very hard cupboard!

The Mouse watches Miss Moppet from the top of the cupboard.

Miss Moppet ties up her head in a duster, and sits before the fire.

The Mouse thinks she is looking very ill. He comes sliding down the bell-pull.

Miss Moppet looks worse and worse. The Mouse comes a little nearer. Miss Moppet holds her poor head in her paws, and looks at him through a hole in the duster. The Mouse comes very close.

And then all of a sudden — Miss Moppet jumps upon the Mouse! And because the Mouse has teased Miss Moppet — Miss Moppet thinks she will tease the Mouse; which is not at all nice of Miss Moppet.

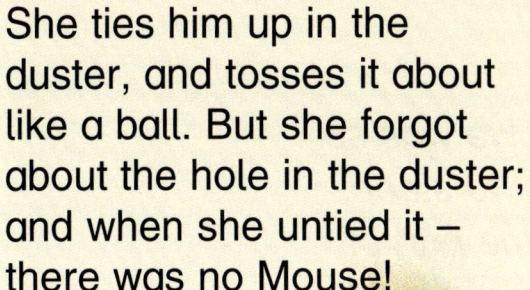

She ties him up in the duster, and tosses it about like a ball. But she forgot about the hole in the duster; and when she untied it – there was no Mouse!

He has wriggled out and run away; and he is dancing a jig on the top of the cupboard!

From More *Tales* by *Beatrix Potter*

The Giant Wakes

Oscar was the last of the giants. He was so lonely that he lay down and went to sleep. Time passed and the giant became part of the land and was called Man Mountain. Matthew and his granddaughter Rose come to live on Man Mountain. Rose goes exploring and wakes the giant ...

Then a Big Voice said: "There's a fly in my mouth!"

And out of the dark of Mouth Cavern came a huge pink soft thing, with Rose sitting on it.

"You're not a fly," the Big Voice said. "You're a person."

"And you're a giant," Rose gasped. "Please don't eat me!"

"I don't eat people!" said the Big Voice.

"Thank you very much," said Rose, standing up and bouncing about.

"Stop tickling!" said the Big Voice.

"I'll just jump off, shall I?" said Rose, and she hopped off into Beard Forest, where she landed in a tree, and had to climb down.

She found Matthew. They clung to each other as the forest rocked and shook. Then the shaking stopped.

"Now we can get away!" Rose said.

But Oscar heard her.

SPLOSH!

A wave came running down Cheek, just missing Rose and Matthew. Then there was another, and another, and another, flooding down off Chin into Chest, and running into Button Lake, washing flowers and grass and rocks and trees with them.

"He's crying!" Rose gasped. "Oh, stop crying, Giant, or everything will be washed away!"

"Can't," said Oscar.

"Why?" said Rose. "Why are you crying?"

"Because if you go away, I'll have no one to talk to," said Oscar.

Rose was sad. She knew what having no one to talk to felt like.

"We won't go away!" she said, bravely.

"Yes we will!" said Matthew.

"No we won't," said Rose. And they didn't.

**From *Man Mountain*
by Martin Waddell**

The Monster Appears

Matty loves her grandma's book of monster stories – even if it is scary!

The following Saturday Matty took the monster book home with her and put it on the bookcase by the side of the bed. Her friend came to play and they played so hard that when Matty went to bed she fell fast asleep just like that.

She woke up. The bright moon was shining through the curtains lighting up the corners of the room, making strange shapes. Matty lay there and watched them. She could see her Wendy House, her blackboard, her railway engine, her teddy bear, her rag doll, all her toys. Her special friends Pink Rabbit and Pobbles the hamster lay beside her on the pillow.

At last she turned to the bookcase by the side of the bed. And as she did so the monster stretched a leg out of the pages, then another leg, then his arms and last of all his dreadful, wicked head.

Matty tried to pull the bedclothes over her but she couldn't. She could only watch as the monster jumped down into the middle of the room.

He began to dance, a horrible dance, waving his horrible arms and horrible legs and shaking his horrible head. Then he leapt onto the top of the Wendy House and stared all round the room. But he did not look at Matty.

As he stood there he started to grow bigger, bigger and BIGGER till he was bigger than Matty. And he laughed a grisly laugh showing all his pointed yellow teeth …

From *Matty's Midnight Monster*

by Gene Kemp

Clever Polly

One day Polly was alone downstairs. Camilla was using the Hoover upstairs, so when the front door bell rang, Polly went to open the door. There was a great black wolf! He put his foot inside the door and said:

"Now I'm going to eat you up!"

"Oh no, please," said Polly. "I don't want to be eaten up."

"Oh, yes," said the wolf, "I am going to eat you. But first tell me, what is that delicious smell?"

"Come down to the kitchen," said Polly, "and I will show you."

There on the table was a delicious-looking pie.

"Have a slice?" said Polly.

The wolf's mouth watered, and he said, "Yes, please!"

Polly cut him a big piece. When he had eaten it, the wolf asked for another, and then for another.

"Now," said Polly, after the third helping, "what about me?"

"Sorry," said the wolf, "I'm too full of pie. I'll come back another day to deal with you."

A week later Polly was alone again, and again the bell rang. Polly ran to open the door. There was the wolf again.

"This time I'm really going to eat you up, Polly," said the wolf.

"All right," said Polly, "but first, just smell."

The wolf took a long breath.

"Delicious!" he said. "What is it?"

"Come down and see," said Polly. In the kitchen was a large chocolate cake.

"Have a slice?" said Polly.

"Yes," said the wolf greedily. He ate six big slices.

"Now, what about me?" said Polly.

"Sorry," said the wolf, "I just haven't got room. I'll come back." He slunk out of the back door.

A week later the door bell rang again. Polly opened the door, and there was the wolf.

"Now this time you shan't escape me!" he snarled. "Get ready to be eaten up now!"

"Just smell all round first," said Polly gently.

"Marvellous!" admitted the wolf. "What is it?"

"Toffee," said Polly calmly. "But come on, eat me up."

"Couldn't I have a tiny bit of toffee first?" asked the wolf. "It's my favourite food."

"Come down and see," said Polly.

The wolf followed her downstairs. The toffee bubbled and sizzled on the stove.

"I must have a taste," said the wolf.

"It's hot," said Polly.

The wolf took the spoon out of the saucepan and put it in his mouth:

OW! HOWL! OW!

It was so hot it burnt the skin off his mouth and tongue and he couldn't spit it out, it was too sticky. In terror, the wolf ran out of the house and never came back!

**From *Clever Polly and the Stupid Wolf*
by Catherine Storr**

Glossary of Verbs

chased	ran after
needed	wanted or required something
robbing	stealing from someone or something
set off	started off
yelled	shouted

clung	hung on to someone or something
gasped	breathe in suddenly when you are shocked or surprised
teased	made fun of or annoyed someone on purpose
wriggled	moved with little twisting movements

admitted	agreed that what someone said was true
leapt	jumped
sizzled	made a hissing sound when cooked
slunk	moving slowly in a guilty way
snarled	growled